SONGS OF THE
1930s

 100 Songs with Online Audio Backing Tracks

W9-DDL-974

To access audio visit:
www.halleonard.com/mylibrary
Enter Code
6492-1036-0824-8278

ISBN 978-1-4950-0026-3

HAL•LEONARD®
CORPORATION
7777 W. BLUEMOUND RD. P.O. BOX 13819 MILWAUKEE, WI 53213

Visit Hal Leonard Online at
www.halleonard.com

ALL OF ME

Words and Music by SEYMOUR SIMONS
and GERALD MARKS

ALL THE THINGS YOU ARE

from VERY WARM FOR MAY

Lyrics by OSCAR HAMMERSTEIN II
Music by JEROME KERN

Time and a-gain I've longed for ad-ven-ture, some-thing to make my heart beat the fast-er. What did I long for? I nev-er real-ly knew. Find-ing your love, I've found my ad-ven-ture;

AND THE ANGELS SING

Lyrics by JOHNNY MERCER
Music by ZIGGY ELMAN

APRIL IN PARIS

Words by E.Y. "YIP" HARBURG
Music by VERNON DUKE

AS TIME GOES BY

from CASABLANCA

Words and Music by
HERMAN HUPFELD

AUTUMN IN NEW YORK

Words and Music by
VERNON DUKE

27

BEGIN THE BEGUINE
from JUBILEE

Words and Music by
COLE PORTER

33

BLAME IT ON MY YOUTH

Words EDWARD HEYMAN
Music by OSCAR LEVANT

BLUE MOON

Music by RICHARD RODGERS
Lyrics by LORENZ HART

BODY AND SOUL

Words by EDWARD HEYMAN,
ROBERT SOUR and FRANK EYTON
Music by JOHN GREEN

CARAVAN

Words and Music by DUKE ELLINGTON,
IRVING MILLS and JUAN TIZOL

CHANGE PARTNERS

from the RKO Radio Motion Picture CAREFREE

Words and Music by
IRVING BERLIN

CHEEK TO CHEEK

from the RKO Radio Motion Picture TOP HAT

Words and Music by
IRVING BERLIN

CHEROKEE
(Indian Love Song)

Words and Music by
RAY NOBLE

DANCING ON THE CEILING
from SIMPLE SIMON

Words by LORENZ HART
Music by RICHARD RODGERS

DANCING IN THE DARK

from THE BAND WAGON and DANCING IN THE DARK

Words by HOWARD DIETZ
Music by ARTHUR SCHWARTZ

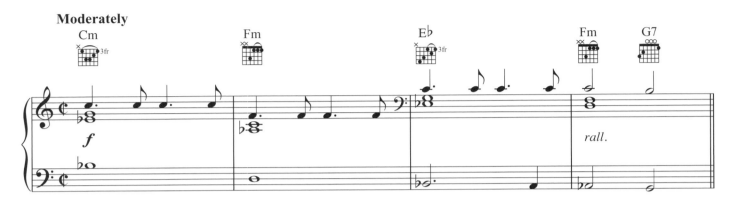

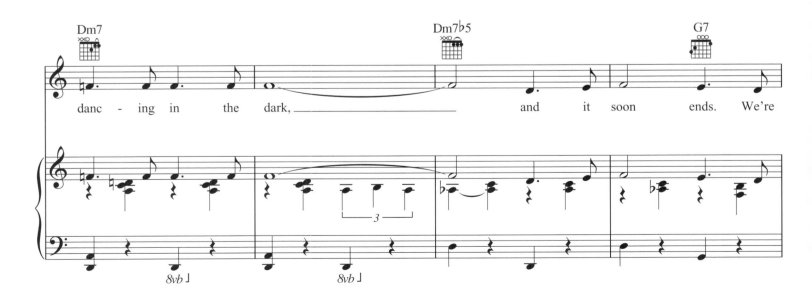

DEEP PURPLE

Words by MITCHELL PARISH
Music by PETER DE ROSE

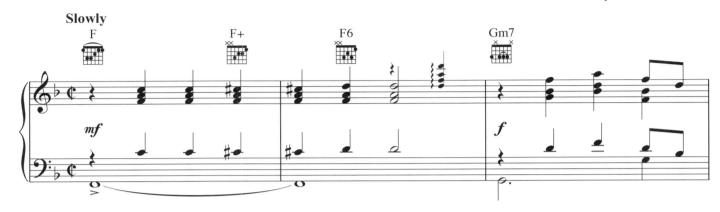

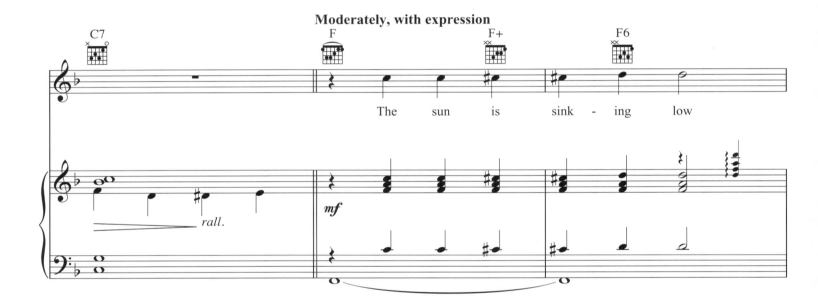

The sun is sink - ing low

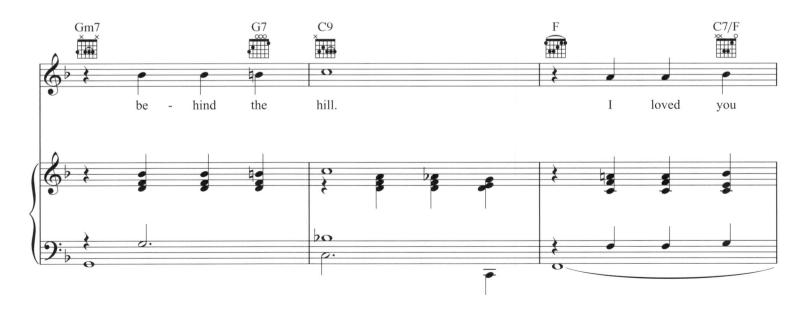

be - hind the hill.   I loved you

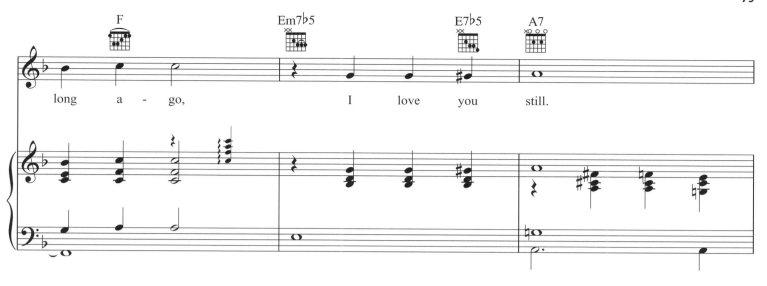

long a - go, I love you still.

A - cross the years you come to me at

twi - light, to bring me love's old

EAST OF THE SUN
(And West of the Moon)

Words and Music by
BROOKS BOWMAN

Slowly, with expression

Lyrics:

East of the sun _____ and west of the moon, _____ we'll build a dream-house _____ of love, dear. Near to the sun in the

EASY LIVING
Theme from the Paramount Picture EASY LIVING

Words and Music by LEO ROBIN
and RALPH RAINGER

EASY TO LOVE
(You'd Be So Easy to Love)
from BORN TO DANCE

Words and Music by
COLE PORTER

EMBRACEABLE YOU

from CRAZY FOR YOU

Music and Lyrics by GEORGE GERSHWIN
and IRA GERSHWIN

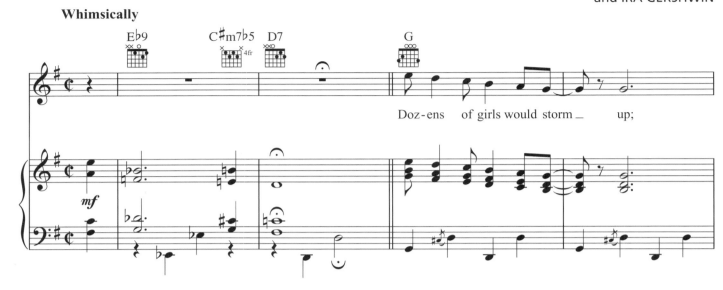

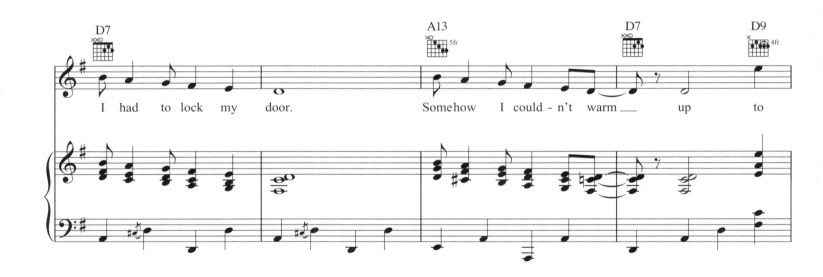

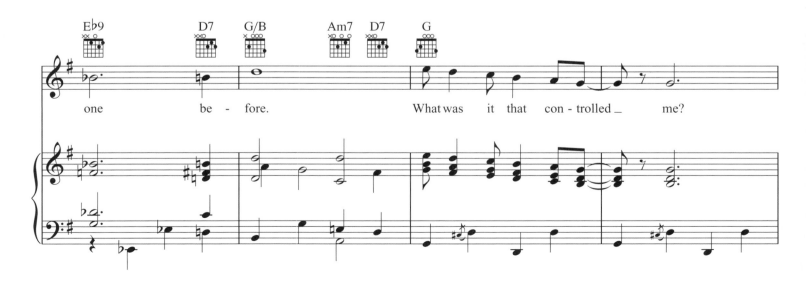

FALLING IN LOVE WITH LOVE
from THE BOYS FROM SYRACUSE

Words by LORENZ HART
Music by RICHARD RODGERS

A FINE ROMANCE

from SWING TIME

Words by DOROTHY FIELDS
Music by JEROME KERN

A FOGGY DAY
(In London Town)
from A DAMSEL IN DISTRESS

Music and Lyrics by GEORGE GERSHWIN
and IRA GERSHWIN

THE FOLKS WHO LIVE ON THE HILL

from HIGH, WIDE AND HANDSOME

Lyrics by OSCAR HAMMERSTEIN II
Music by JEROME KERN

115

GOODY GOODY

Words by JOHNNY MERCER
Music by MATT MALNECK

Moderately bright and swingy

GEORGIA ON MY MIND

Words by STUART GORRELL
Music by HOAGY CARMICHAEL

(Geor - gia on my mind.) Geor - gia, _____ Geor - gia, _____ a song of you comes as sweet and clear as moon - light through the pines. _____ Oth - er arms _ reach out to me; ___ Oth - er eyes ___ smile ten - der - ly; ___

GLAD TO BE UNHAPPY
from ON YOUR TOES

Words by LORENZ HART
Music by RICHARD RODGERS

THE GLORY OF LOVE

Words and Music by
BILLY HILL

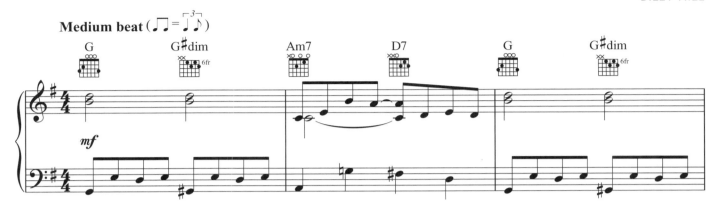

You've got to give a lit-tle,

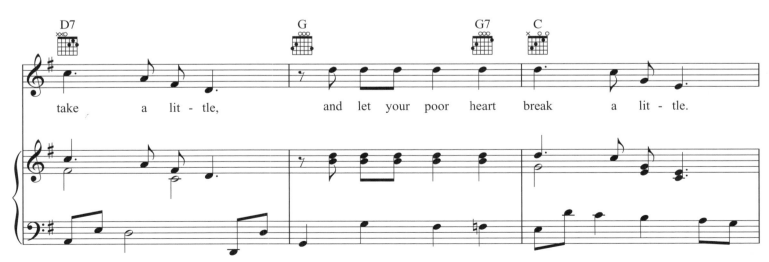

take a lit-tle, and let your poor heart break a lit-tle.

HOW DEEP IS THE OCEAN
(How High Is the Sky)

Words and Music by
IRVING BERLIN

Lyrics:
How much do I love you? I'll tell you no lie, how deep is the o-cean, how high is the sky? How man-y

I CONCENTRATE ON YOU

from BROADWAY MELODY OF 1940

Words and Music by
COLE PORTER

I CAN'T GET STARTED

from ZIEGFELD FOLLIES

Words by IRA GERSHWIN
Music by VERNON DUKE

I DON'T KNOW WHY
(I Just Do)

Lyric by ROY TURK
Music by FRED E. AHLERT

145

I DON'T STAND A GHOST OF A CHANCE WITH YOU

Words by BING CROSBY and NED WASHINGTON
Music by VICTOR YOUNG

I ONLY HAVE EYES FOR YOU

from DAMES

Words by AL DUBIN
Music by HARRY WARREN

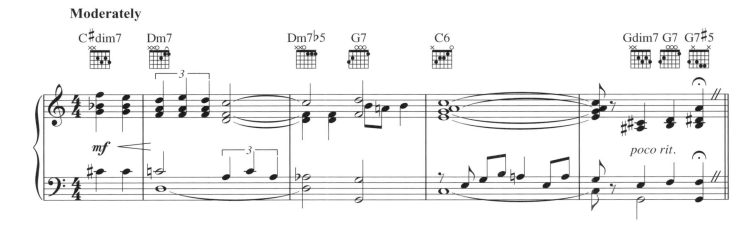

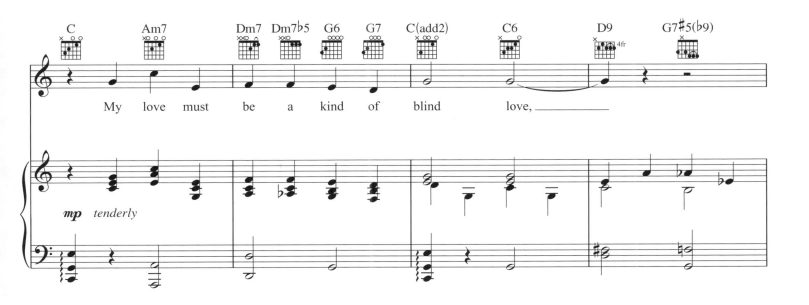

My love must be a kind of blind love, _____

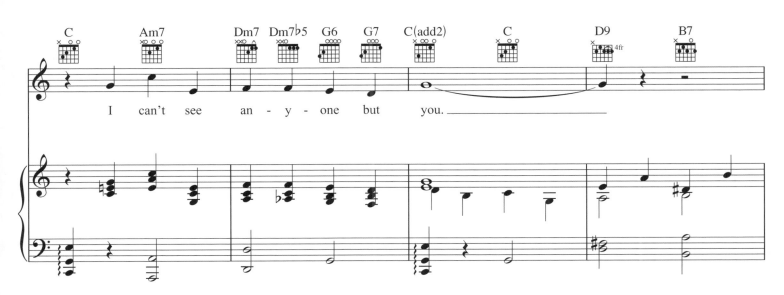

I can't see an-y-one but you. _____

And dear, I won-der if you find love

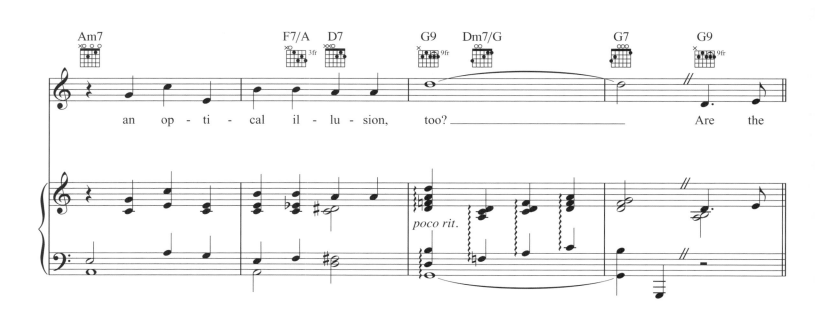

an op-ti-cal il-lu-sion, too? _____ Are the

poco rit.

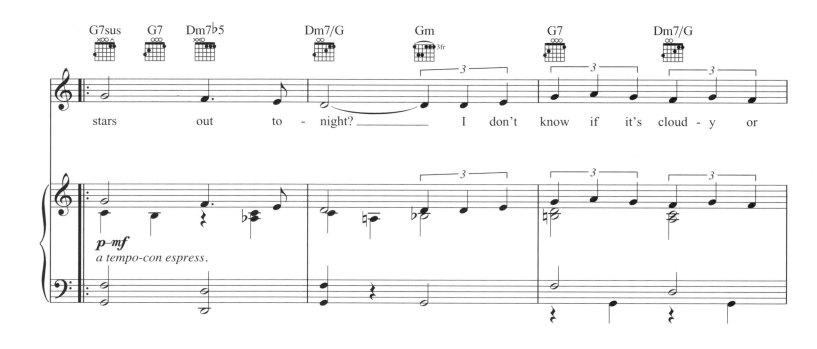

stars out to - night? _____ I don't know if it's cloud-y or

p–mf
a tempo-con espress.

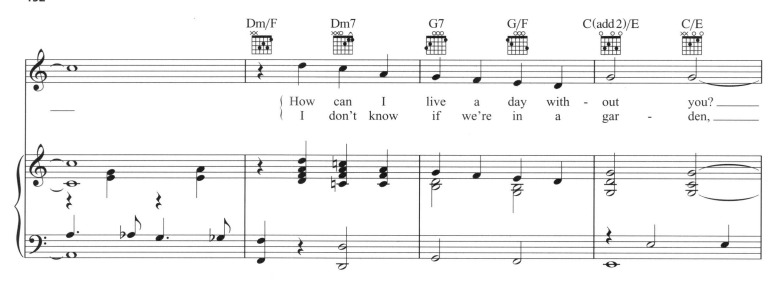

How can I live a day with - out you? _____
I don't know if we're in a gar - den, _____

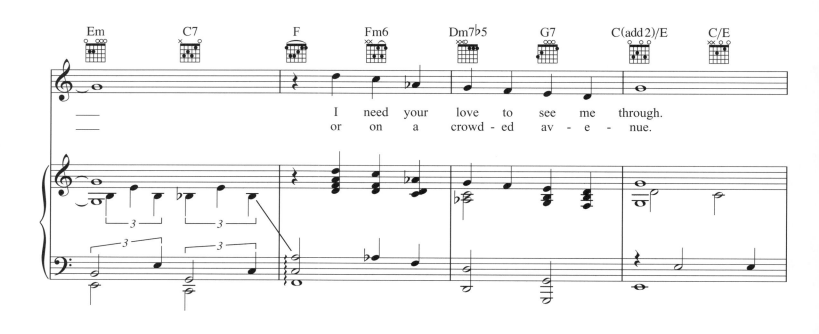

_____ I need your love to see me through.
_____ or on a crowd - ed av - e - nue.

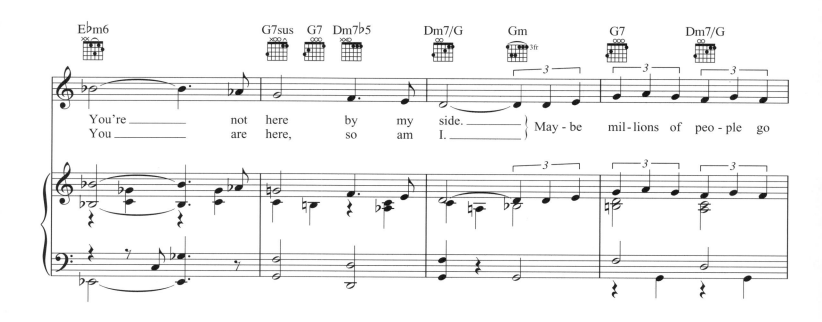

You're _____ not here by my side. _____ May - be mil - lions of peo - ple go
You _____ are here, so am I. _____

by. _____ But they all dis - ap - pear _____ from

view. _____ And I on - ly have eyes _____ for

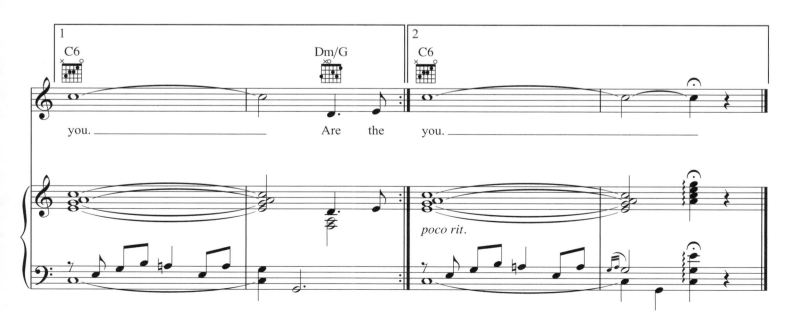

you. _____ Are the you. _____

poco rit.

I GOT RHYTHM

from AN AMERICAN IN PARIS
from GIRL CRAZY

Music and Lyrics by GEORGE GERSHWIN
and IRA GERSHWIN

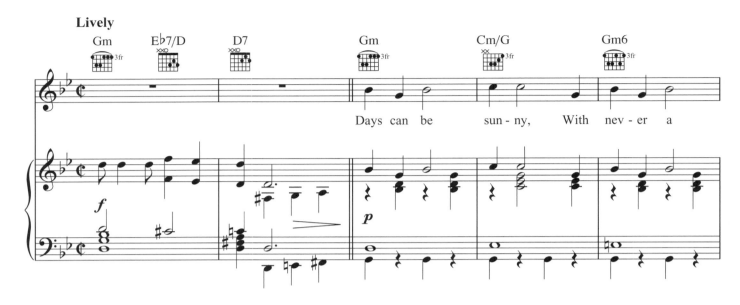

Lively

Days can be sun - ny, With nev - er a

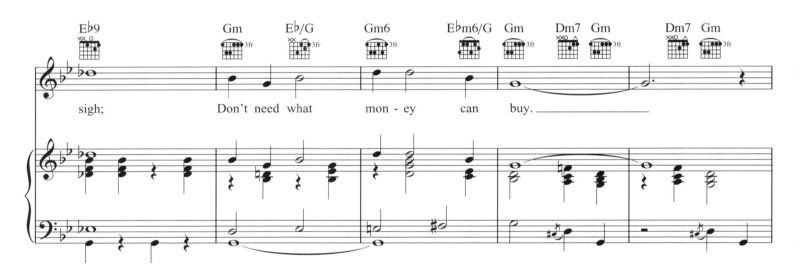

sigh; Don't need what mon - ey can buy. ____

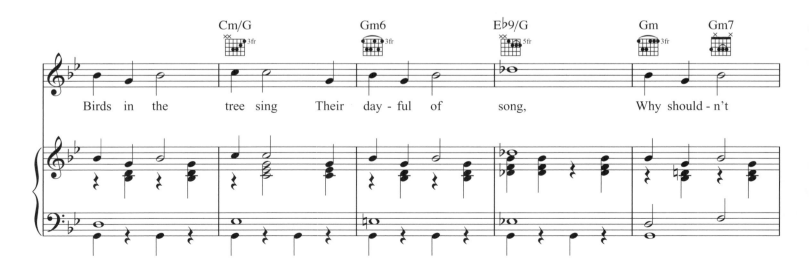

Birds in the tree sing Their day - ful of song, Why should - n't

I WON'T DANCE

from ROBERTA

Words and Music by JIMMY McHUGH, DOROTHY FIELDS,
JEROME KERN, OSCAR HAMMERSTEIN II
and OTTO HARBACH

I'LL BE SEEING YOU

from RIGHT THIS WAY

Written by IRVING KAHAL
and SAMMY FAIN

find you in the morn - ing sun; and when the night is

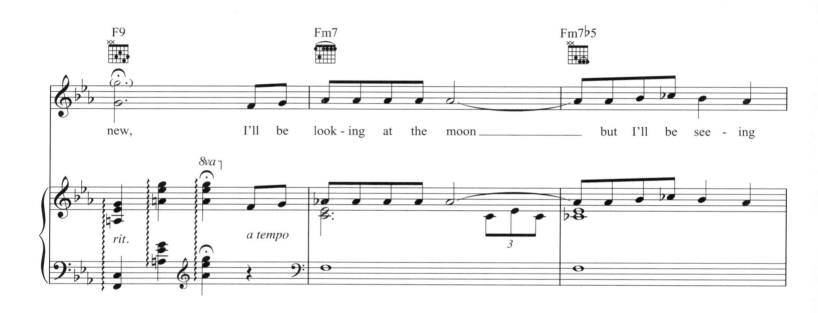

new, I'll be look - ing at the moon _____ but I'll be see - ing

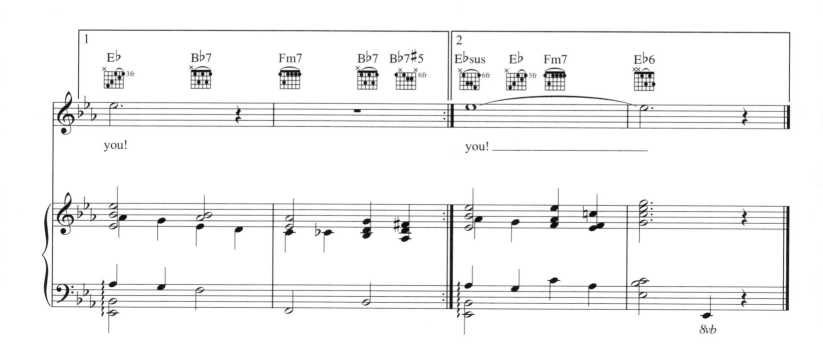

you! you! _____

I'M CONFESSIN'
(That I Love You)

Words and Music by AL NEIBURG,
DOC DAUGHERTY and ELLIS REYNOLDS

I'm con- fess- in' that I love you.

Tell me, do you love me too? I'm con- fess- in' that I

need you, hon- est I do, need you ev- 'ry mo- ment.

I'M IN THE MOOD FOR LOVE

from EVERY NIGHT AT EIGHT

Words and Music by JIMMY McHUGH
and DOROTHY FIELDS

I'M GETTING SENTIMENTAL OVER YOU

Words by NED WASHINGTON
Music by GEORGE BASSMAN

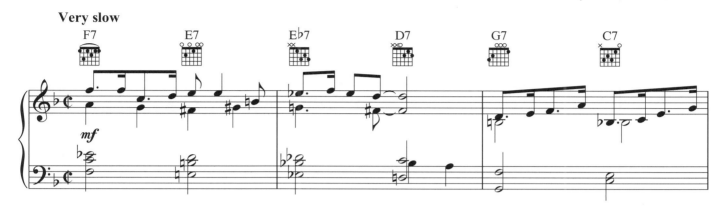

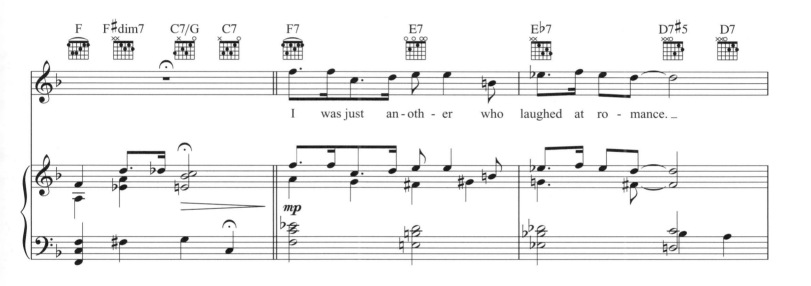

I was just an-oth-er who laughed at ro-mance.

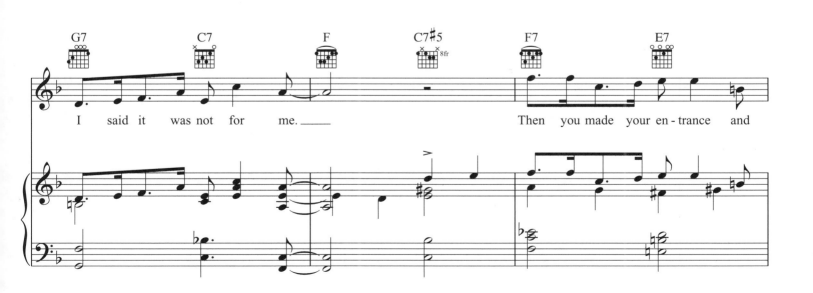

I said it was not for me. Then you made your en-trance and

176

I'VE GOT MY LOVE TO KEEP ME WARM

from the 20th Century Fox Motion Picture ON THE AVENUE

Words and Music by
IRVING BERLIN

I'VE GOT THE WORLD ON A STRING

Lyric by TED KOEHLER
Music by HAROLD ARLEN

I'VE GOT YOU UNDER MY SKIN
from BORN TO DANCE

Words and Music by
COLE PORTER

IN A SENTIMENTAL MOOD

Words and Music by DUKE ELLINGTON,
IRVING MILLS and MANNY KURTZ

ISN'T IT ROMANTIC?

from the Paramount Picture LOVE ME TONIGHT

Words by LORENZ HART
Music by RICHARD RODGERS

197

Cm   G7#5   Cm   Eb7/Bb   Ab   C7/G

in the trees a - bove.   While
or she'll get the sack.   And

Fm   Bb7 Bdim7   Cm   F9   Bbdim7   Bb7

all the world is say - ing you were meant for love. Is - n't it ro -
when I take a show - er, she can scrub my back. Is - n't it ro -

Eb   Bb7   Eb   Bb7#5

man - tic? Mere - ly to be young on such a night as
man - tic? On a moon - light night she'll cook me on - ion

Eb   Bb7   Eb   Bb7

this? Is - n't it ro - man - tic? Ev - 'ry note that's sung is
soup. Kid - dies are ro - man - tic, and if we don't fight, we

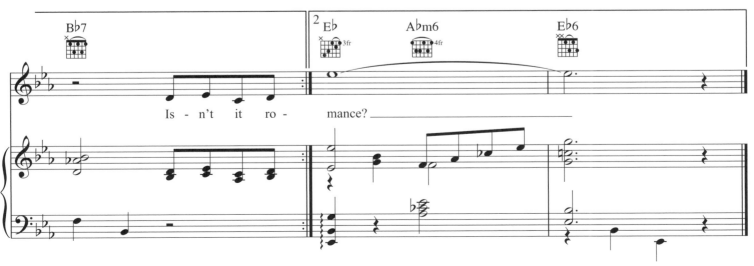

IN THE MOOD

By JOE GARLAND

IN THE STILL OF THE NIGHT

from ROSALIE
from NIGHT AND DAY

Words and Music by
COLE PORTER

207

IT DON'T MEAN A THING
(If It Ain't Got That Swing)

Words and Music by DUKE ELLINGTON
and IRVING MILLS

IT'S DE-LOVELY
from RED, HOT AND BLUE!

Words and Music by
COLE PORTER

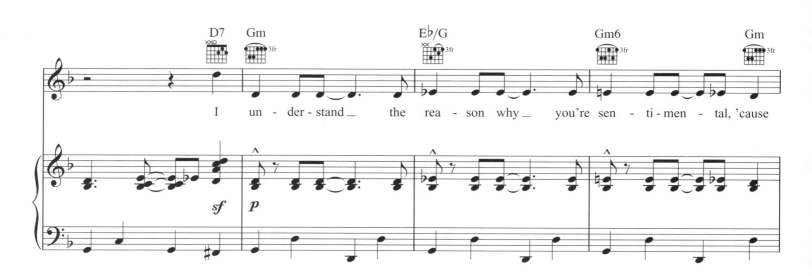

Lyrics:
The night is young, the skies are clear and if you want to go walk-ing, dear, it's de-light-ful, it's de-li-cious, it's de-love-ly. I un-der-stand the rea-son why you're sen-ti-men-tal, 'cause

215

IT'S EASY TO REMEMBER

from the Paramount Picture MISSISSIPPI

Words by LORENZ HART
Music by RICHARD RODGERS

IT'S ONLY A PAPER MOON

featured in the Motion Picture TAKE A CHANCE

Lyric by BILLY ROSE and E.Y. "YIP" HARBURG
Music by HAROLD ARLEN

JUST ONE MORE CHANCE

Words by SAM COSLOW
Music by ARTHUR JOHNSTON

THE LADY IS A TRAMP

from BABES IN ARMS
from WORDS AND MUSIC

Words by LORENZ HART
Music by RICHARD RODGERS

LAZY RIVER

from THE BEST YEARS OF OUR LIVES

Words and Music by HOAGY CARMICHAEL
and SIDNEY ARODIN

LET'S CALL THE WHOLE THING OFF

from SHALL WE DANCE

Music and Lyrics by GEORGE GERSHWIN
and IRA GERSHWIN

Allegretto

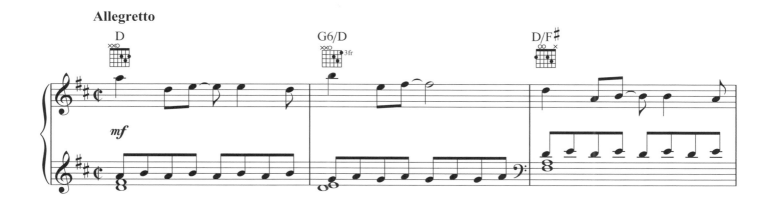

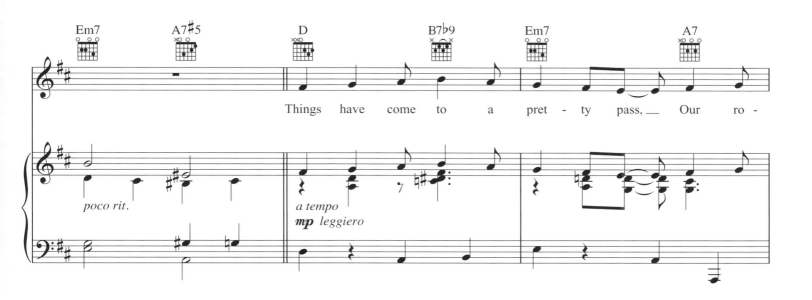

Things have come to a pret-ty pass,__ Our ro-

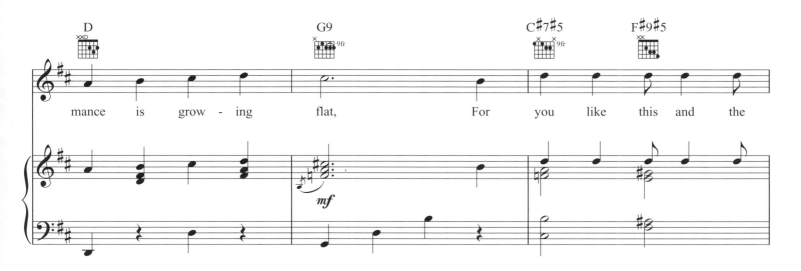

mance is grow-ing flat, For you like this and the

LET YOURSELF GO

from the Motion Picture FOLLOW THE FLEET

Words and Music by
IRVING BERLIN

LET'S FALL IN LOVE

Words by TED KOEHLER
Music by HAROLD ARLEN

247

LITTLE GIRL BLUE
from JUMBO

Words by LORENZ HART
Music by RICHARD RODGERS

luck - y lit - tle girl blue.

Sit there and count the rain - drops fall - ing on

you. It's time you knew,

all you can count on is the rain - drops That

LOVER

from the Paramount Picture LOVE ME TONIGHT

Words by LORENZ HART
Music by RICHARD RODGERS

LOVE IS HERE TO STAY

from AN AMERICAN IN PARIS
from GOLDWYN FOLLIES

Music and Lyrics by GEORGE GERSHWIN
and IRA GERSHWIN

LOVE WALKED IN

Music and Lyrics by GEORGE GERSHWIN
and IRA GERSHWIN

LULLABY OF BROADWAY

from GOLD DIGGERS OF 1935
from 42ND STREET

Words by AL DUBIN
Music by HARRY WARREN

LULLABY OF THE LEAVES

Words by JOE YOUNG
Music by BERNICE PETKERE

Rus-tling of the leaves used to be my lull-a-by,

THE NEARNESS OF YOU

from the Paramount Picture ROMANCE IN THE DARK

Words by NED WASHINGTON
Music by HOAGY CARMICHAEL

MOOD INDIGO

Words and Music by DUKE ELLINGTON,
IRVING MILLS and ALBANY BIGARD

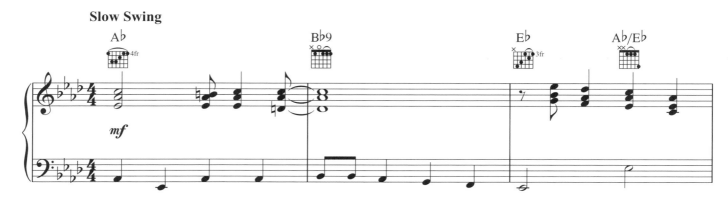

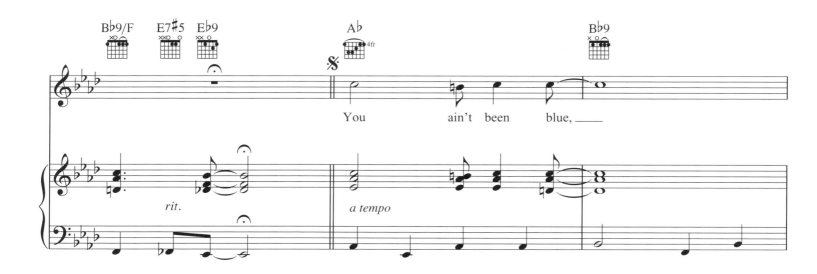

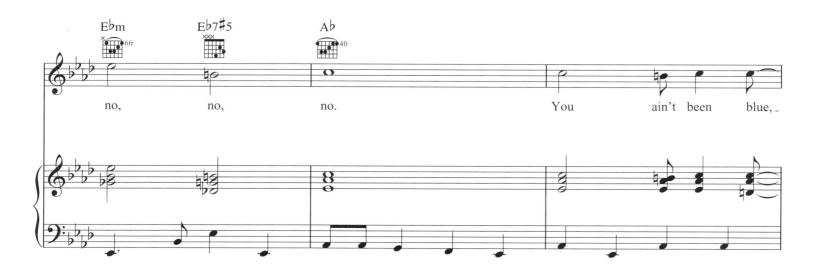

MOONGLOW

Words and Music by WILL HUDSON,
EDDIE DE LANGE and IRVING MILLS

MY FUNNY VALENTINE

from BABES IN ARMS

Words by LORENZ HART
Music by RICHARD RODGERS

MY ROMANCE

from JUMBO

Words by LORENZ HART
Music by RICHARD RODGERS

NEVERTHELESS
(I'm in Love with You)

Words and Music by BERT KALMAR
and HARRY RUBY

fine at the start, __ then left with a heart __ that is break -

ing. May - be I'll live __ a life of re - gret __ and

may - be I'll give __ much more than I'll get, __ but nev - er - the - less, __ I'm in

love with you. _____

NICE WORK IF YOU CAN GET IT
from A DAMSEL IN DISTRESS

Music and Lyrics by GEORGE GERSHWIN
and IRA GERSHWIN

The man who on-ly lives for mak-ing mon-ey

Lives a life that is-n't nec-es-sar-i-ly sun-ny. Like-wise the man who

works for fame, There's no guar-an-tee that time won't e-rase his

NIGHT AND DAY

from GAY DIVORCE
from THE GAY DIVORCEE

Words and Music by
COLE PORTER

ON THE SUNNY SIDE OF THE STREET

Lyric by DOROTHY FIELDS
Music by JIMMY McHUGH

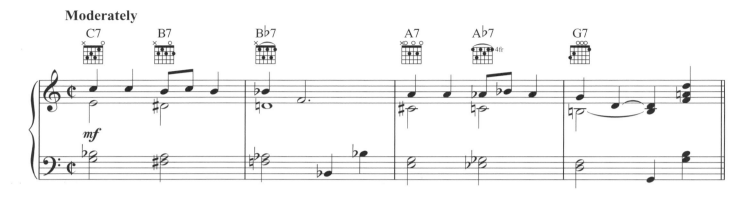

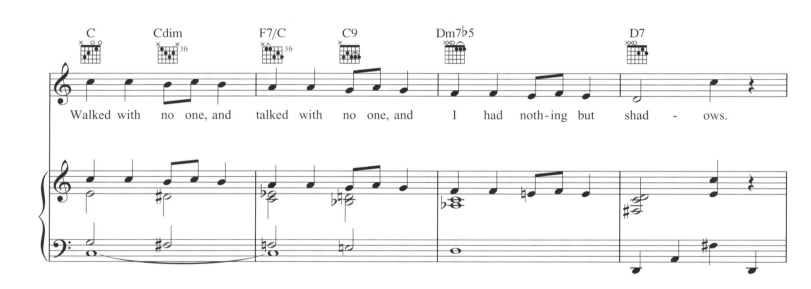

Walked with no one, and talked with no one, and I had noth-ing but shad-ows.

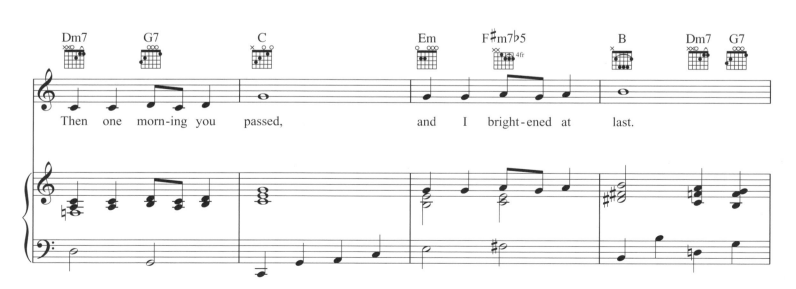

Then one morn-ing you passed, and I bright-ened at last.

ONCE IN A WHILE

Words by BUD GREEN
Music by MICHAEL EDWARDS

OVER THE RAINBOW

from THE WIZARD OF OZ

Music by HAROLD ARLEN
Lyric by E.Y. "YIP" HARBURG

fly. Birds fly o - ver the rain - bow, why then, oh why can't

I? I?

hap - py lit - tle blue-birds fly be - yond the rain - bow, why oh why can't I?

PENNIES FROM HEAVEN

from PENNIES FROM HEAVEN

Words by JOHN BURKE
Music by ARTHUR JOHNSTON

PICK YOURSELF UP

from SWING TIME

Words by DOROTHY FIELDS
Music by JEROME KERN

SEPTEMBER SONG
from the Musical Play KNICKERBOCKER HOLIDAY

Words by MAXWELL ANDERSON
Music by KURT WEILL

SING, SING, SING

Words and Music by
LOUIS PRIMA

SMOKE GETS IN YOUR EYES

from ROBERTA

Words by OTTO HARBACH
Music by JEROME KERN

SOLITUDE

Words and Music by DUKE ELLINGTON,
EDDIE DE LANGE and IRVING MILLS

STOMPIN' AT THE SAVOY

Words by ANDY RAZAF
Music by BENNY GOODMAN,
EDGAR SAMPSON and CHICK WEBB

STARS FELL ON ALABAMA

Words by MITCHELL PARISH
Music by FRANK PERKINS

Moon - light and mag - no - lia, star - light in your hair,

STORMY WEATHER
(Keeps Rainin' All the Time)
from COTTON CLUB PARADE OF 1933

Lyric by TED KOEHLER
Music by HAROLD ARLEN

SUMMERTIME

from PORGY AND BESS®

Music and Lyrics by GEORGE GERSHWIN,
DuBOSE and DOROTHY HEYWARD
and IRA GERSHWIN

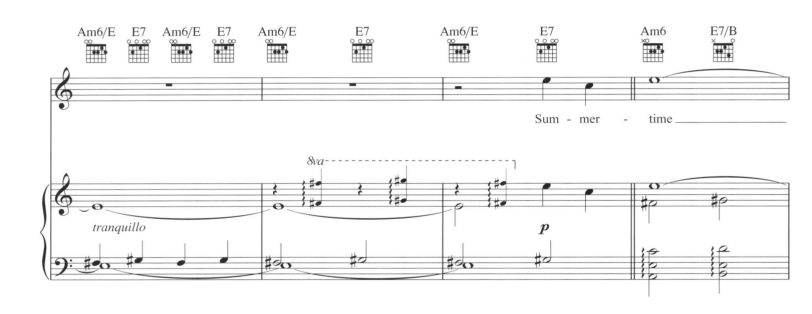

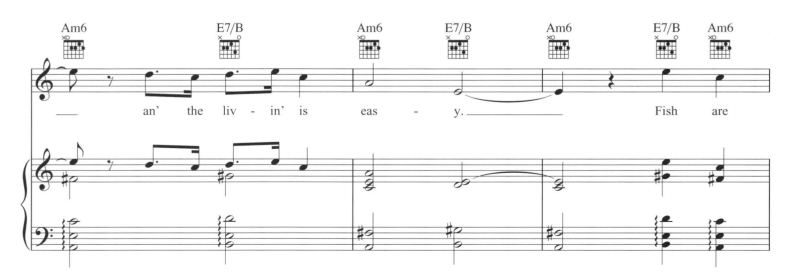

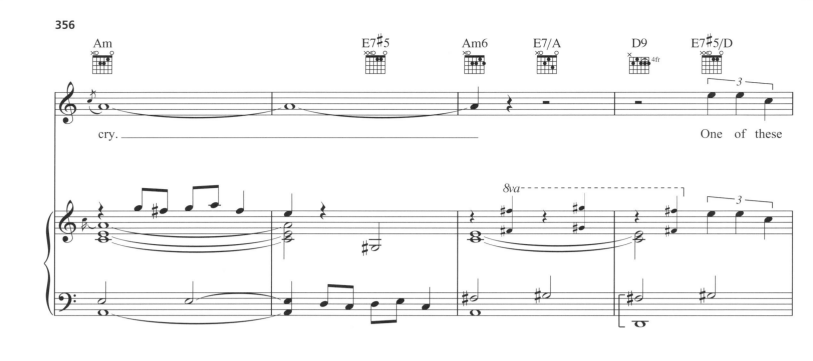

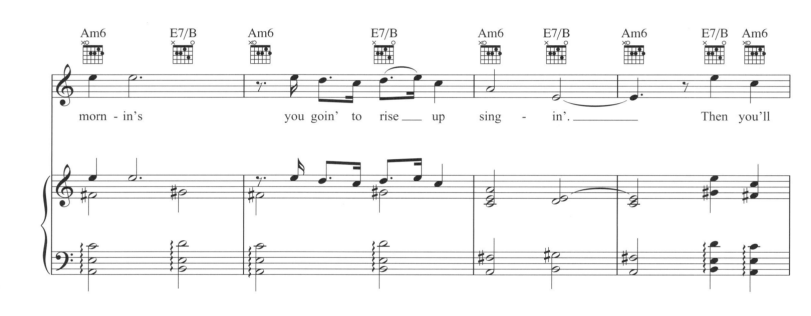

TEN CENTS A DANCE

from SIMPLE SIMON

Words by LORENZ HART
Music by RICHARD RODGERS

THESE FOOLISH THINGS
(Remind Me of You)

Words by HOLT MARVELL
Music by JACK STRACHEY

THANKS FOR THE MEMORY
from the Paramount Picture BIG BROADCAST OF 1938

Words and Music by LEO ROBIN
and RALPH RAINGER

THERE IS NO GREATER LOVE

Words by MARTY SYMES
Music by ISHAM JONES

THEY CAN'T TAKE THAT AWAY FROM ME

from SHALL WE DANCE
from THE BARKLEYS OF BROADWAY

Music and Lyrics by GEORGE GERSHWIN
and IRA GERSHWIN

THIS CAN'T BE LOVE
from THE BOYS FROM SYRACUSE

Words by LORENZ HART
Music by RICHARD RODGERS

THREE LITTLE WORDS

from the Motion Picture CHECK AND DOUBLE CHECK

Lyric by BERT KALMAR
Music by HARRY RUBY

THE VERY THOUGHT OF YOU

Words and Music by
RAY NOBLE

THE WAY YOU LOOK TONIGHT

from SWING TIME

Words by DOROTHY FIELDS
Music by JEROME KERN

WHAT A LITTLE MONLIGHT CAN DO

Words and Music by
HARRY WOODS

WHAT IS THIS THING CALLED LOVE?

from WAKE UP AND DREAM

Words and Music by
COLE PORTER

Moderately

I was a hum-drum per-son, leading a life a-part, when
You gave me days of sun-shine, you gave me nights of cheer, when you

love flew in through my win-dow wide, and quick-ened my hum-drum heart.
made my life an en-chant-ed dream, till some-bod-y else came near.

Love flew in through my win-dow, I was so hap-py then. But
Some-bod-y else came near you, I felt the win-ter's chill. And

WHERE OR WHEN

from BABES IN ARMS

Words by LORENZ HART
Music by RICHARD RODGERS

When you're a-wake the things you think come from the dreams you dream.

Thought has wings, _____ and lots of things _____ are sel-dom what they seem.

Some-times you think you've lived be-fore, all that you live to - day.

WRAP YOUR TROUBLES IN DREAMS
(And Dream Your Troubles Away)

Lyric by TED KOEHLER and BILLY MOLL
Music by HARRY BARRIS

YOU'RE GETTING TO BE A HABIT WITH ME

from 42ND STREET

Lyrics by AL DUBIN
Music by HARRY WARREN

YOU MUST HAVE BEEN
A BEAUTIFUL BABY

Words by JOHNNY MERCER
Music by HARRY WARREN

Does your moth-er re-al-ize the stork de-liv-ered quite a prize, the day he left you on the fam-'ly tree?

Does your dad ap-pre-ci-ate that you are mere-ly su-per great, the mir-a-cle of an-y cen-tu-